Colo

Green

Gabrielle Woolfitt

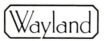

COLOURS

Blue
Green
Red
Yellow

First published in 1991 by
Wayland (Publishers) Limited
61 Western Road, Hove
East Sussex BN3 1JD, England

© Copyright 1991 Wayland (Publishers) Limited

Editor: Cath Senker
Designer: Derek Lee

Consultant: Tom Collins, Deputy Headmaster of St Leonards CEP School, East Sussex

British Library Cataloguing in Publication Data
Woolfitt, Gabrielle
Green. – (Colours)
I. Title II. Series
372.3

ISBN 0-7502-0187 8

Typeset by Kalligraphic Design Ltd, Horley, Surrey
Printed by G. Canale & C.S.p.A. Turin
Bound by Casterman, S.A. Belgium

Words printed in **bold** are explained in the glossary.

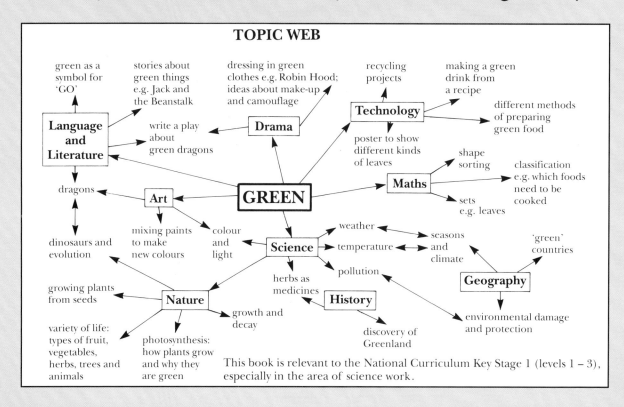

This book is relevant to the National Curriculum Key Stage 1 (levels 1 – 3), especially in the area of science work.

CONTENTS

WHAT IS GREEN?	4
GREEN FOR GO	6
GREEN IN NATURE	8
GREEN COUNTRIES	10
GREEN GROWTH	12
GREEN ANIMALS	14
GREEN STORIES	16
UNRIPE GREEN	18
GREEN FOOD	20
COOL GREEN	22
GREEN HERBS	24
GREEN WORLD	26
GREEN MONSTERS	28
PROJECTS	30
GLOSSARY	31
BOOKS TO READ	31
INDEX	32

WHAT IS GREEN?

Green is a natural colour. Plants and trees are green. Lots of vegetables are green. Emeralds are green precious stones.

You can make green by mixing yellow and blue paint. Try adding blue to yellow paint. Only add a little each time. Watch the colour change from lime green
to leaf green
and then to bottle green.

People also make green things. This boy is playing with green toys. What do you have in your home that is green?

GREEN FOR GO

Green is a safety colour. Green means go. The green man signal at the pedestrian crossing means it is safe to cross the road – but always keep looking!

There is a green sign in this picture. What does it mean?

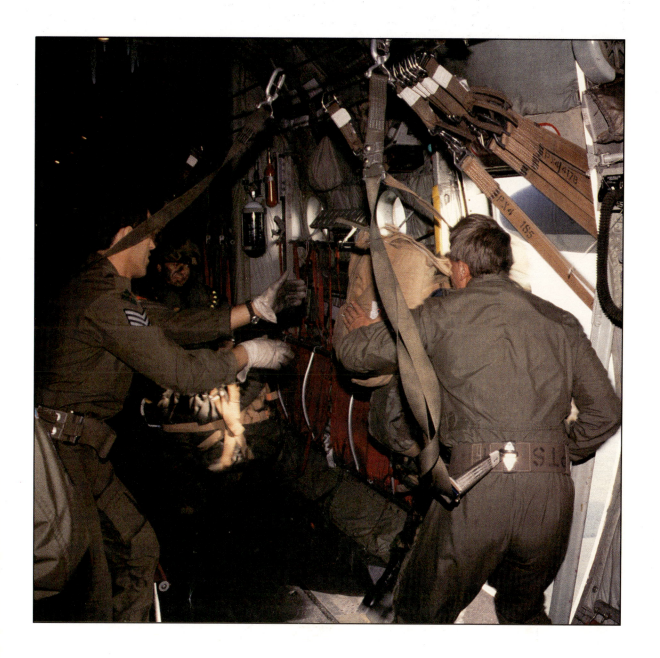

These men are in an aeroplane. They have **parachutes** on their backs. Can you see the green light? The green light goes on when it is time to jump out.

GREEN IN NATURE

Walk through a park on a sunny day. Look at the plants and trees. All of them have green leaves. Why?

Plants make their own food in their leaves. They need sunlight, air and water. They can only **absorb** the sunlight if their leaves are green.

Collect some different leaves. Find out which leaf comes from which kind of plant. Make a poster to show what you have found out.

oak

ash

maple

sycamore

GREEN COUNTRIES

These beautiful green fields are in Ireland. It rains a lot in Ireland. The rain helps the grass to grow. Ireland is sometimes called the Emerald **Isle** because it is so green.

This is Greenland. It is a very cold, snowy island. The **Viking** explorer who discovered it wanted people to come and live here. He called it Greenland to make it sound nice. The people who first came here were tricked!

Find out about other places with green in the name, such as Greenwich.

GREEN GROWTH

In winter it is cold. The ground is hard. There are only a few hours of sunlight each day. Plants do not grow.

At the end of winter, tiny green shoots begin to poke through the earth. They grow into plants.

These flowers are snowdrops.

Soon new green shoots grow on bushes. Green buds grow on trees. Flowers grow from the buds. Seeds begin to grow into plants. Spring is here.

GREEN ANIMALS

There are many green animals. Some jump, some fly, and some crawl along the ground. These parrots have wings. They fly.
   Think of some other green animals. How do they move?

Can you see the animal in this picture? The chameleon is green like the tree. It is hard to see. A bigger animal might want to eat the chameleon. But is it easy to find?

GREEN STORIES

Do you know the story of Jack and the beanstalk? The beanstalk grows from a magic bean. When Jack climbs up the beanstalk he meets a fierce giant. Find out what happens next.

Have you heard the story of Robin Hood? He lived in Sherwood Forest with his friends. They took money from rich people and gave it to poor people.

The rich people tried to stop them. But the forest was green and Robin Hood and his friends wore green clothes. Why do you think it was hard to catch them?

UNRIPE GREEN

Most fruits and **cereals** are green while they are growing. They are **unripe**. Even oranges are green when they are unripe! As they ripen in the sun, they change colour. Then they are ready for picking.

You could not eat this corn. It needs more sunlight to help it to ripen. What colour will the corn be when it is ripe?

Bananas are picked when they are still green. They are sent on ships to the countries that buy them. When they arrive they have turned yellow. They are ready to eat.

GREEN FOOD

Sometimes food is green because it is unripe. Sometimes it is green because it is **mouldy**.

But most green food is meant to be green. Look at these green foods.
Which kinds of green food can you eat raw?
Which green foods could you put in a salad?
Which green foods taste sweet?

Make a chart to show which green foods your friends like best.

COOL GREEN

Green is a colour that can make you feel cool on a hot summer day. You can sit in the cool green shade of a leafy tree.

This sea anemone is cooling down in a cool green pool.

Here is a recipe for a cool green summer drink.

1. Mix lime cordial with lemonade in a jug.
2. Put some ice cubes in each glass.
3. Pour in the drink. Decorate with a **sprig** of mint.
4. Add a slice of fresh lime to each glass.

GREEN
HERBS

Many different herbs grow in this garden.

Herbs are special plants that are used for their taste and **aroma**. Herbs have strong flavours. They can make food and drink taste delicious.

Mint tea is a very popular drink in Arab countries. Mint can be made into sauce and served with roast lamb.

Some herbs make oils which smell nice. Rosemary oil is used in some shampoos.

Other herbs can be used as medicines. Camomile helps people to sleep.

mint

rosemary

camomile

GREEN
WORLD

Your home and the places nearby are your environment. Every person, animal and plant needs a clean environment.

Pollution makes the environment dirty. **Litter** is pollution. Car **exhaust** pollutes the air. Pollution can kill living things. People who look after their environment are often called 'the greens'.

Some ways to be a green:
1. Don't drop litter.
2. Take empty glass bottles to the bottle bank.
3. Use **recycled** paper and reuse plastic bags.

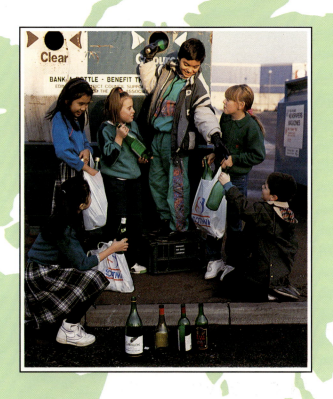

Children using a bottle bank.

GREEN
MONSTERS

Millions of years ago dinosaurs lived on the earth. They were very large. Some dinosaurs were probably green. The dinosaurs have been **extinct** for a long time.

An iguanodon

Dragons look rather like dinosaurs. But dragons are only make-believe. Lots of people tell stories about dragons.
Some dragons in stories are fierce and breathe fire. Others eat people.
Some dragons are very old and wise.
Others can fly.
Some dragons collect treasure.
Make up a play about a dragon.

PROJECTS

Please ask an adult to help you with the projects.

Growing mung bean seeds

1. Put some loose soil in a pot.
2. Make holes in the soil about 2 cm apart, using a pencil.
3. Put one mung bean seed in each hole.
4. Cover the seeds with soil.
5. Water the seeds so the soil is damp.
6. Put the pot in a warm place.
7. Remember to water the seeds a little every day.
8. Watch your plants grow.

Recycling project

Collect aluminium drink cans. The cans are aluminium if they do not stick to a magnet. You can sell aluminium cans. Write to this address to find out more:

Aluminium Can Recycling Association
1 Mex House
52 Blucher Street
Birmingham B1 1QU

Tel. 021 633 4656

GLOSSARY

Absorb To soak up, like a sponge.
Aroma A nice smell.
Cereal A grain plant, such as wheat, maize or rice.
Exhaust The used gas that comes out of a car.
Extinct No longer existing, like the dinosaurs.
Isle Another word for island.
Litter Rubbish.
Mouldy Something that has a furry growth on it because it has gone bad.
Parachute A large piece of cloth shaped like an umbrella, used to slow down the fall of someone jumping from an aircraft.
Pollution Something that poisons the environment.
Recycle To reuse.
Sprig A shoot from a plant.
Unripe Not ready for picking or eating.
Vikings Fierce sailors who lived about a thousand years ago.

BOOKS TO READ

The Enchanted World: Dragons (Time Life Books, 1985)
Herbs and Spices by Linda Illsley (Wayland, 1990)
Spring Weather by John Mason (Wayland, 1990)
The Young Green Consumer Guide by J. Elkington and J. Hailes (Gollancz, 1990)

PICTURE ACKNOWLEDGEMENTS

The photographs in this book were provided by: Heather Angel 12; Angus Blackburn 27; Chapel Studios 20–21; Bruce Coleman COVER, 15; Eye Ubiquitous 11 (top); Trevor Hill 5, 23; Hutchison 14, 19, 22, 24; The Research House 7; Topham 6, 16, 17, 18; Zefa 8, 10–11. Artwork: Jenny Hughes imprint page, 4–5, 26–7; Peter Lubach 29; Colin Newman 28; John Yates 9, 12–13, 16, 17, 25.

INDEX

Numbers in **bold** refer to illustrations.

aeroplane **7**

bananas 19
bottle bank 26–7
buds 13

camomile 25
chameleon 15
corn 18

dinosaurs 28
dragons 29
drink recipe 23

environment 26–7

fruit 18–19, **20–21**

Greenland 11
the greens 26

Ireland 10

Jack and the
   beanstalk 16

leaves 8–9

mint 25

painting 4
parrots 14
plants 12
pollution 26

recycling 26, 30
Robin Hood 17
rosemary 25

sea anemone 22
snowdrops **12**
spring 13

toys **5**
traffic signals 6
tree **8**

vegetables **20–21**

winter 12

CHILDREN OF ST. MARTHA
SCHOOL LIBRARY